MILAN 2013

THE CITY AT A GLANCE

Chiesa di San Babila

On the site of a Roman templ[e]
to the 2nd century, this churc[h]
by Saint Babila, the Bishop o[f]
rebuilt at the end of the 11th
Piazza San Babila

GW00585255

Quadrilatero della Moda

This is where to splash your
end Italian fashion boutiques that line via
Alessandro Manzoni, Via Montenapoleone,
Via della Spiga and Via Sant'Andrea.

Torre Velasca

In the immediate vicinity of the Duomo, this
arresting 1950s structure pays an inverted
compliment to its medieval neighbour.
See p011

Palazzo Arcivescovile

The Archbishop's Palace has undergone
much restructuring over the years. The 16th-
century architect Pellegrino Pellegrini's
sophisticated decagonal stables and inner
courtyard make it well worth a visit.
Via dell'Arcivescovado

Duomo

It's the sheer scale of Milan's restored 14th-
century cathedral, one of the biggest in
the world, that will cause you to pause for
a moment. Big really can be beautiful.
See p014

Galleria Vittorio Emanuele II

Given a new lease of life by the opening of
chic shops and the TownHouse Street Duomo
hotel (see p020) under its spectacular roof,
Giuseppe Mengoni's 19th-century Galleria is
one of Europe's most elegant arcades.
See p013

INTRODUCTION
THE CHANGING FACE OF THE URBAN SCENE

Depending on your perspective, Milan is either in the south of the north of Europe, or in the north of the south – making the Milanese, with their proximity to the borders of Switzerland, Austria and France, a different breed from their cousins in the rest of Italy. Unlike Rome, Venice or Florence, Milan doesn't offer all its visual wares on a plate, so you'll have to work harder to discover the city's gems. Many people come for its design events, including Milan Fashion Week and the highly influential furniture show, Salone Internazionale del Mobile, which takes place every April. During the latter, the city is transformed, as each available space is turned into a showroom. These fairs provide a great excuse for a visit, although not if you want to secure a good hotel rate.

Other visitors are likely to land in Milan for the sensational shopping – there's no better place, as the most tempting boutiques are close together and sell coveted items that you probably won't be able to find elsewhere. Things got even better when Galleria Vittorio Emanuele II (see p013) underwent a luxe renaissance, and Gucci, Tod's and Louis Vuitton moved in to join Prada (see p068). More recently, a spate of new and revamped stores has opened on Via Montenapoleone. Milan's hotels (see p016) are better now than they have ever been, and incorporate some of the most enticing spas in the world. After all, this is a city fixated by style, where looking your best is absolutely king.

ESSENTIAL INFO

FACTS, FIGURES AND USEFUL ADDRESSES

TOURIST OFFICE
Milano è Turismo
Piazza Castello 1/Via Beltrami
T 02 7740 4343
www.turismo.milano.it

TRANSPORT
Car hire
Avis
Piazza Armando Diaz 6
T 02 8901 0645
Metró
T 800 808 811
www.atm-mi.it
Trains run daily from 6am to 12.30am
Taxis
Radio Taxi
T 02 4040
Cabs can't be hailed in the street. Pick
one up at a taxi rank or book in advance

EMERGENCY SERVICES
Ambulance
T 118
Fire
T 115
Police
T 113
24-hour pharmacy
Stazione Centrale Farmacie
Galleria della Partenze
T 02 669 0735

CONSULATES
British Consulate
Via San Paolo 7
T 02 723 001
www.ukinitaly.fco.gov.uk
US Consulate
Via Principe Amedeo 2-10
T 02 290 351
milan.usconsulate.gov

POSTAL SERVICES
Post office
Via Cordusio 4
T 02 7248 2126
www.poste.it
Shipping
Mail Boxes Etc
T 02 7210 5005

BOOKS
A Traveller in Italy by HV Morton
(Methuen)
Gio Ponti by Ugo La Pietra (Rizzoli
International Publications)

WEBSITES
Art/Design
www.brera.beniculturali.it
Newspapers
www.corriere.it
www.repubblica.it

EVENTS
Cortili Aperti
www.adsi.it
MiArt
www.miart.it
Salone Internazionale del Mobile
www.cosmit.it

COST OF LIVING
**Taxi from Linate Airport
to city centre**
€25
Cappuccino
€2
Packet of cigarettes
€4
Daily newspaper
€1.20
Bottle of champagne
€70

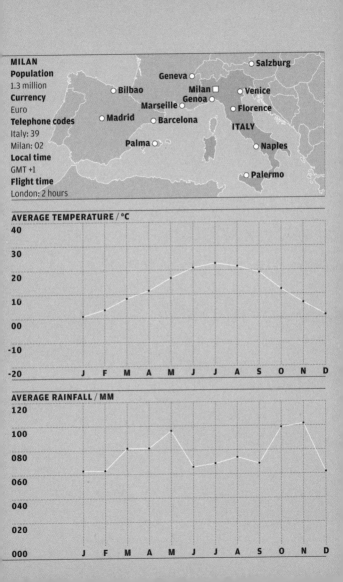

MILAN
Population
1.3 million
Currency
Euro
Telephone codes
Italy: 39
Milan: 02
Local time
GMT +1
Flight time
London: 2 hours

Salzburg
Geneva
Bilbao
Milan
Venice
Marseille
Genoa
Madrid
Florence
Barcelona
ITALY
Palma
Naples
Palermo

AVERAGE TEMPERATURE / °C

40
30
20
10
00
-10
-20

J F M A M J J A S O N D

AVERAGE RAINFALL / MM

120
100
080
060
040
020
000

J F M A M J J A S O N D

NEIGHBOURHOODS

THE AREAS YOU NEED TO KNOW AND WHY

To help you navigate the city, we've chosen the most interesting districts (see below and the map inside the back cover) and colour-coded our featured venues, according to their location; those venues that are outside these areas are not coloured.

MAGENTA

The oldest *pasticceria* in Milan, and still one of the best, Pasticceria Marchesi (Via Santa Maria alla Porta 11a, T 02 862 770), is just down the road from the convent of Santa Maria delle Grazie, in which *The Last Supper* hangs. The city's chicest district, Magenta has great local shops, including design gallery Spazio Rossana Orlandi (see p044). Visit the Museo Archeologico (Corso Magenta 15, T 02 8844 5208) for its architecture and ancient artefacts.

SEMPIONE

Leading out from the back of Castello Sforzesco (see p009) is Parco Sempione, where Gio Ponti constructed Torre Branca (see p012), and designer Achille Castiglioni based his studio, which is now a fascinating museum (see p032). To the west is one of the city's finest cafés, Leonardo (Via Aurelio Saffi 7, T 02 439 0302), and Stazione di Cadorna, from where trains run every 30 minutes to Malpensa Airport.

ZONA DUOMO/GALLERIA

Linking Piazza del Duomo and Piazza della Scala is Galleria Vittorio Emanuele II (see p013), Milan's magnificent shopping arcade. Emerge from its stylish promenades to face the overwhelming Duomo (see p014). Nearby, Museo del Novecento (see p062) displays a splendid selection of modern Italian art. Umberto Boccioni, Giorgio de Chirico and Lucio Fontana are some of the artists whose work you will see.

QUADRILATERO DELLA MODA

Milan's famed 'Golden Triangle' has a plethora of beautiful boutiques, many of which have received an architect-designed revamp during the past few years. The shopping area has segued into Via Verri, San Pietro All'Orto and Corso Venezia, where you'll find design store De Padova (see p078). The neighbourhood is also home to some classic Milan venues such as the Four Seasons hotel (see p017) and the restaurant Il Baretto al Baglioni (see p048).

BRERA

Beginning just behind La Scala (Piazza della Scala, T 02 8879), the Brera district is concentrated on Via Brera and Via Fiori Chiari, and has several galleries selling works by salient designers such as Gio Ponti and Angelo Mangiarotti, among others. Two excellent examples are the Anna Maria Consadori Gallery (see p077) and Erastudio (see p035), which focuses on both designers and architects.

ZONA TORTONA

During Salone del Mobile, this area is the most important circuit *fuori salone*, 'outside the fair', teeming with the HQs of the big brands, including the monumental Teatro Armani on Via Bergognone, which was designed by Tadao Ando. Also here are Renzo Rosso's Diesel, Ermenegildo Zegna's modernist offices by Antonio Citterio and Gianmaria Beretta, and restaurant Circle (Via Enrico Stendhal 36, T 02 4229 3745).

LANDMARKS

THE SHAPE OF THE CITY SKYLINE

Milan's historic nucleus is around the Duomo (see p014), from which a star of arteries radiates through the modern suburbs to the ring road. Next to the cathedral is Galleria Vittorio Emanuele II (see p013), and a few minutes south, through Piazza Armando Diaz, you will spy the outlandish Torre Velasca (see p011). In the south-west lies the Navigli area, where there are a few remaining canals that once were part of a system of navigable rivers. Behind Porta Genova station, this is the location of Zona Tortona, a former industrial area now populated by numerous design companies. Castello Sforzesco (Piazza Castello, T 02 8846 3700) lies north-west of the cathedral and leads to Parco Sempione, home of the Milan Triennale (see p032) and Gio Ponti's Torre Branca (see p012).

Milan's layout is changing, though, thanks to regeneration schemes like Progetto Porta Nuova, which can be seen emerging above the traditional houses of Corso Como. Designed by several architects, including Pelli Clarke Pelli and Kohn Pedersen Fox, the project will link the Garibaldi, Varesine and Isola areas with a series of walkways and a large park, and encompass new civic, residential, cultural and commercial buildings. The most distinctive structure is Boeri Studio's Bosco Verticale (Vertical Forest), a pair of high-rise apartment blocks planted with some 900 trees – the aim being to combat pollution and foster energy efficiency.
For full addresses, see Resources.

Pirelli Tower

This iconic 32-storey building, near Stazione Centrale, is proof positive that a modernist skyscraper need not result in repetitive banality. Built for Pirelli, the tyre manufacturer, it was completed in 1958, and was the tallest building in Italy at the time. Its architect, Gio Ponti, was joined by many collaborators on the project, including engineer Pier Luigi Nervi, and the building helped shape Ponti's future career. Unable to meet its huge running costs, Pirelli sold the building to the regional government of Lombardy in 1973, which was housed here until its offices relocated to Palazzo Lombardia (see p058) in 2011. Il Pirellone, as it is fondly referred to locally, was completely refurbished after a small plane famously flew into it in 2002.
Piazza Duca d'Aosta 3

Torre Velasca

Much debated at home and abroad at the time of its construction, the 1958 Torre Velasca was designed by BBPR (Gian Luigi Banfi, Lodovico Barbiano di Belgiojoso, Enrico Peressutti and Ernesto Nathan Rogers). A remarkable take on a medieval fortress, it swells at the residential upper storeys, resembling a watchtower, and its cantilevered supports are an inverted nod to the Duomo's famous buttresses (see p014). The spacing of the windows is irregular, creating interesting patterns on the facade. Torre Velasca's lobby is open to the public but the rest of the building is off-limits. After a stroll around the surrounding plaza, visit the nearby Rotonda della Besana (Via Enrico Besana 15), a late baroque church with beautiful porticoes, now used as a cultural venue. *Piazza Velasca 5*

Torre Branca

Towering over Parco Sempione, next door to the Milan Triennale (see p032), stands Torre Branca, an elegant 108.6m metal tower. It was designed by Cesare Chiodi, Ettore Ferrari and Gio Ponti in 1933, as part of an exhibition for the fifth Triennale (at that time, exhibitions were held once every three years, hence the name). Originally owned by Distillerie Branca, it now belongs to the Comune di Milano.

For €4 you can ride up to the viewing platform. If you have a head for heights you'll be rewarded with a great view of the city, although patience may be required, as the lift carries only seven at a time and visitors have to descend before the next in line are allowed up. Opening hours can be erratic, so call before you visit.
Viale Luigi Camoens, Parco Sempione,
T 02 331 4120

Galleria Vittorio Emanuele II

Architect Giuseppe Mengoni's double arcade was both innovative and daring for its time, and remains influential to this day. One of the world's first shopping centres, the Galleria was constructed between 1865 and 1877 as two four-storey promenades, with mosaicked floors and a vaulted iron and glass roof. It swiftly became a fashionable place to shop, as well as a symbol of the belle époque.

A victim of bomb damage during WWII, the building underwent a major refurbishment in the 1960s, including a total renovation of the floor. More recently, it has enjoyed a contemporary renaissance, with hotels (see p020) and luxury designer stores opening inside. To maintain the superior appearance, every retailer has to agree to having a gold sign on a black background. *Piazza del Duomo/Piazza della Scala*

Duomo

Although it was commissioned in 1386 by Gian Galeazzo Visconti, the world's fourth-largest cathedral was only completed in the early 1800s (locals joke it was 1960). A surprisingly elegant mass of marble, it features more than 100 spires and thousands of statues. An extensive restoration of the facade was unveiled in 2010.
Piazza del Duomo

HOTELS

WHERE TO STAY AND WHICH ROOMS TO BOOK

In the mid-noughties, the accommodation scene in Milan was turned on its head. The Antonio Citterio-designed Bulgari Hotel (see po28), set in a former monastery surrounded by spectacular gardens; Park Hyatt (see po25), which has suites designed by Ed Tuttle; and neighbouring Straf (see po18), the debut hotel from architect/designer Vincenzo De Cotiis, set a new standard in this ultra-style-conscious city. Following on their heels, the Armani Hotel (see po26) – a 95-room realisation of the fashion designer's aesthetic inside a 1937 rationalist building – Palazzo Segreti (see po22) and the stylish TownHouse Street Duomo (see po20) have since added a much-needed boutique element.

If your taste veers more towards the traditional, the Four Seasons (opposite), housed in a 15th-century convent, and Grand Hotel et de Milan (see po24), where Giuseppe Verdi lived for almost 30 years, are impeccable choices. Just outside the city, another venerable option is the restored Hotel Villa San Carlo Borromeo (see po30), which has long hosted artists and writers, including Leonardo da Vinci and Stendhal. And there are more hotels to come. In late 2013, a Mandarin Oriental (Via Monte di Pietà) opens in a redevelopment of three elegant 19th-century buildings close to Quadrilatero della Moda, and, the following year, a W (Via Brera 19, T 02 63 361) will hold court in trendy Brera. *For full addresses and room rates, see Resources.*

Dear Reader, books by Phaidon are recognized worldwide for their beauty, scholarship and elegance. We invite you to return this card with your name and e-mail address so that we can keep you informed of our new publications, special offers and events. Alternatively, visit us at **www.phaidon.com** to see our entire list of books, videos and stationery. Register on-line to be included on our regular e-newsletters.

Subjects in which I have a special interest

☐ General Non-Fiction   ☐ Art   ☐ Photography   ☐ Architecture   ☐ Design

☐ Fashion   ☐ Music   ☐ Children's   ☐ Food   ☐ Travel

	Mr/Miss/Ms	Initial	Surname
Name			
No./Street			
City			
Postcode/Zip code		Country	
E-mail			

This is not an order form. To order please contact Customer Services at the appropriate address overleaf.

Please delete address not required before mailing

PHAIDON PRESS LIMITED

Regent's Wharf

All Saints Street

London N1 9PA

UK

PHAIDON PRESS INC.

180 Varick Street

New York

NY 10014

USA

Return address for USA and Canada only

Return address for UK and countries outside the USA and Canada only

Four Seasons

Opened in 1993, the Four Seasons remains popular with visitors enamoured by its proximity to Milan's shopping district, and its unique setting. The hotel is laid out across a former convent, and the best of its 118 rooms, including the Renaissance Suite (above), surround the magnificent cloistered courtyard. Other recommended rooms include Suites 14, 16, 18 and 19, all of which are split-level. The work of Filippo Peroni, a set designer for La Scala (see p053) in the 1800s, can be viewed in the lounge and Camino room, while the lobby is a refined spot in which to unwind. In winter, the hotel opens an extravagant Chocolate Room, lined with all manner of cocoa-inspired delights. As is customary at a Four Seasons, service is exemplary. *Via Gesù 6-8, T 02 77 088, www.fourseasons.com/milan*

Straf

The 64-room Straf (short for San Raffaele) is conveniently positioned next door to Galleria Vittorio Emanuele II (see p013), in a converted 19th-century palazzo. For his first hotel project, Milan-based Vincenzo De Cotiis, whose CV includes a string of retail projects, chose a combination of materials – burnished brass, iron, slate, etched glass and cement, some of which are recycled (there's an eco-conscious ethos to many of Straf's services). The result is a kind of gentle brutalism, as seen in the Standard Room (above), softened by works of modern art. There's no spa as such, but several rooms have Japanese auto-massage chairs. The bar draws a crowd come *aperitivo*, and Straf hosts various arts events during the year. *Via San Raffaele 3, T 02 805 081, www.straf.it*

3Rooms

When the former journalist Carla Sozzani opened the bar/restaurant/shop/gallery 10 Corso Como in 1991 (think a more sophisticated version of Colette in Paris), it was an instant success that single-handedly transformed the once edgy area around Stazione Garibaldi. Today, Corso Como is still worth the pilgrimage. The tiny (the clue is in the name) and upmarket bed-and-breakfast property that Sozzani opened on the site in 2003 has had a more mixed reception. There can be no doubting the elegance of the rooms, such as No 3 (above), and tasteful furnishings by the likes of Eero Saarinen and Arne Jacobsen, but it is fair to say that your chances of securing a reservation may depend a little too much on who you are.
Corso Como 10, T 02 626 163,
www.3rooms-10corsocomo.com

TownHouse Street Duomo
This 2012 addition to the TownHouse group of hotels occupies the first and second floors of a refurbished office building near the Duomo (see p013). Yellow, black and white are the principal colours in the four studios and three double rooms (Two-bedroom Suite, pictured), by Italian architect Simone Micheli. A butler service is available.
Via Santa Radegonda 14, T 02 8905 8297

Palazzo Segreti

Tucked down a quiet street just steps from Castello Sforzesco (see p009), Palazzo Segreti lives up to its name as a rather 'secret' address. Set in a late 19th-century building, this seductive boutique hotel, whose interior was conceived by owners Roberta and Francesco Tibaldi together with architects Brizzi+Riefenstahl Studio, pairs exposed brick and concrete with warm wooden floors and soft furnishings in the 18 unique rooms and lobby (opposite). The three suites, including Room 8 (above), benefit from large baths in the bedroom areas. Breakfast consists of a selection of regional produce; a refreshing change from the usual sugary brioche. Charcuterie, local cheeses and Italian wines are served in the lounge bar. *Via San Tomaso 8, T 02 4952 9250, www.palazzosegreti.com*

Grand Hotel et de Milan

Favoured by opera devotees (Giuseppe Verdi lived here from 1872 until his death in 1901, and Maria Callas made it her home while she was performing at La Scala), the Grand has a historic aura, its distinctive neo-Gothic facade overlooking the intersection of Via Manzoni and Via Montenapoleone. In the late 1800s, it was the only hotel in the city able to provide postal and telegraphic services, drawing diplomats, dignitaries and politicians through its doors. Following WWII, the US army requisitioned the entire hotel. The decor is a medley of styles, ranging from 18th-century through to Liberty and art deco; many of the rooms have been refurbished by Dimore Studio, including the elegant Suite Superior (above).
Via Alessandro Manzoni 29, T 02 723 141, www.grandhoteletdemilan.it

Park Hyatt

A contemporary classic carved out of a late 19th-century palazzo, the Park Hyatt, opened in 2003, neighbours the Duomo (see p014) and La Scala (see p053). A muted colour scheme, travertine stone and sumptuous fabrics create a lavish yet sleek feel, in both the Ed Tuttle-designed suites and other rooms, which all have the advantage of generously sized bathrooms. The outdoor terrace of the Park Bar, on one of Milan's few pedestrianised streets, is a prime place to people watch, as is La Cupola (above), the lobby/lounge with a sculpture by Argentina-born Italian artist Lucio Fontana. Opt for Rooms 105 or 205, overlooking Galleria Vittorio Emanuele II (see p013), or if money is no object, the Diplomatic Suite, which has a large terrace. *Via Tommaso Grossi 1, T 02 8821 1234, www.milan.park.hyatt.com*

Armani Hotel
After launching in Dubai, Giorgio Armani chose Enrico A Griffini's modernist Milan building for his second hotel venture: a 95-room property in the heart of the city. Most of the public areas (lobby, pictured) are situated on the seventh and eighth floors in the glass 'hat', which affords a terrific panorama. The spa (see p092) is as chic a temple to wellbeing as you'd expect.
Via Alessandro Manzoni 31, T 02 8883 8381

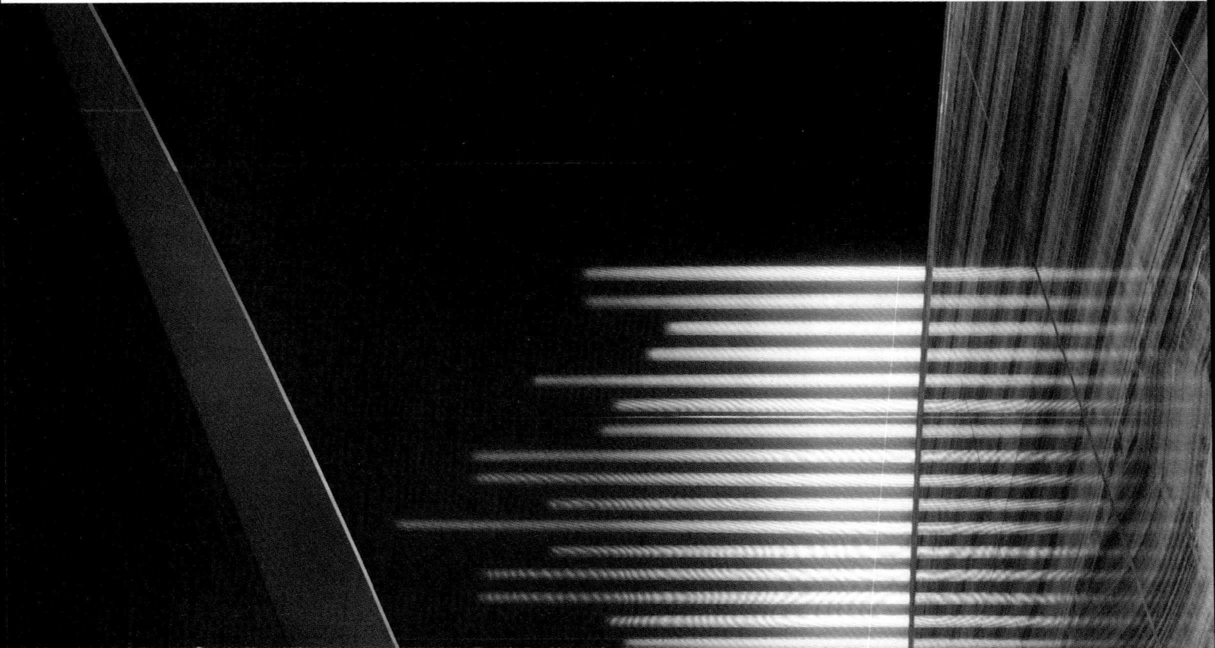

Bulgari Hotel

Bulgari opened this, its first hotel, as a joint venture with the Marriott group in 2004. Several years on, its contemporary luxury remains a lure for the city's fashion and design set. Antonio Citterio chose oak, bronze and matt black marble as key elements of the decor, and many of the 58 rooms exploit the sensational setting overlooking a 4,000 sq m garden backing on to Milan's Orto Botanico; we suggest a Deluxe Suite (above). The hotel's serene interior and grounds belie its location less than five minutes' walk from Via Montenapoleone. The impressive day spa, which includes a Turkish bath set in an emerald-glass cube, and a pool lined with gold mosaic, is worth a half-day visit whether you are a guest at the hotel or not. During summer, the terrace bar (opposite) is a stylish choice for *aperitivo*.
Via Privata Fratelli Gabba 7b,
T 02 805 8051, www.bulgarihotels.com

Hotel Villa San Carlo Borromeo

Located 12km from the centre of Milan in Senago, San Carlo Borromeo's storied past is believed to stretch back more than a thousand years. It's thought Julius Caesar used the hilltop site as a Roman stronghold; centuries later, Leonardo da Vinci is said to have visited the palatial residence that was subsequently built here. Today, after a specialist restoration spanning several decades, the villa exudes a grandeur and refinement, as seen in the first-floor hall (above), fitting for its rich history. The hotel and its 51 rooms and suites feature intricate frescoes, mosaics, rococo Venetian furniture and artworks, and have views that take in the rolling, statue-studded gardens. There's also a museum, showing Renaissance art. *Piazza Borromeo 20, Senago, T 02 994 741, www.hotelvillasancarloborromeo.com*

Foresteria Monforte

This charming, affordable *foresteria* (guest house) is a little gem, in a central, largely residential area of the city, five minutes' walk to Piazza San Babila. The amenities are geared towards the self-sufficient traveller (there's no reception or room service) but breakfast is served in the rooms and guests can access a communal kitchen. There are three airy rooms – two standard, including Centrale (above), and one suite – all overlooking a square, and the decor in each one is a judicious blend of contemporary and antique furnishings. Owners Giovanni Zonca and Gianni Aporti converted a first-floor apartment above their pharmacy to create Monforte, and its relaxed, affable feel is a real draw. The hotel fills up fast, so book well in advance. *Piazza del Tricolore 2, T 02 370 272, www.foresteriamonforte.it*

24 HOURS

SEE THE BEST OF THE CITY IN JUST ONE DAY

Milan's rich design history is the focus of our day, which could, of course, also be happily spent in the boutiques of Via della Spiga, Via Sant'Andrea and Via Montenapoleone. After *caffè* and brioche at contemporary café Pavè (opposite), we recommend a visit to one of the city's historic houses, the achingly elegant Villa Necchi Campiglio (see p034), and its beautiful gardens. Next we head to Brera, to design and architecture gallery Erastudio (see p035). Should you need fortifying en route, stop for a *panzerotto* at local institution Luini (Via Santa Radegonda 16, T 02 8646 1917).

Before lunch, we stop off at Studio Museo Achille Castiglioni (Piazza Castello 27, T 02 805 3606), where the lauded designer worked for 40 years until his death in 2002. Now a museum, it offers a rare opportunity to gain an insight into the processes behind Castiglioni's work (Tuesday to Saturday 10am-1pm; visits by appointment). Nearby, the Milan Triennale (Viale Alemagna 6, T 02 724 341) has a permanent collection of Italian design, as well as temporary exhibitions, and is next door to Gio Ponti's Torre Branca (see p012). To the east, Fondazione Vico Magistretti (see p036) is another studio museum devoted to a seminal designer.

Aperitivo is *di rigore* in Milan – call in at Ama.mi (see p052) any time from 5.30pm to 10.30pm, before a classic Milanese dinner at the immaculate Il Salumaio di Montenapoleone (see p038). *For full addresses, see Resources.*

09.00 Pavè

Three friends – Giovanni Giberti, Luca Scanni and Diego Bamberghi – are behind Pavè, which opened in 2012 in the most multicultural area of Milan, close to Corso Buenos Aires. The café/deli has fast gained a reputation for its excellent *pasticcini* and bread, all of which are prepared in-house. Made with stoneground flour, the bread is taken out of the oven every day at 4.30pm, in time for those returning home from work. In the morning, try the brioche with Tahitian vanilla cream, or *sbrisolona*, a traditional Lombardy cake. On Sundays, the scrumptious Millefoglie Express, a puff-pastry cake filled with cream, is made to order. Pavè's eclectic interior is as joyous as the food, and features reclaimed furnishings. Closed Mondays. *Via Felice Casati 27, T 02 9439 2259, www.pavemilano.com*

10.30 Villa Necchi Campiglio

Immortalised in Luca Guadagnino's 2009 film *I Am Love*, this rationalist villa offers a rare glimpse into the lifestyle of Milan's great industrialists. The owners were sisters Gigina and Nedda Necchi, and Gigina's husband, Angelo Campiglio, manufacturers of cast iron and enamel sewing machines from the 1920s to the 1960s, and renowned for their chic parties. Built between 1932 and 1935, the villa was designed by Milanese architect Piero Portaluppi, and converted into a museum in 2008. The interiors are a sumptuous combination of rich walnut, marble and antiques, and Claudia Gian Ferrari's collection of early 20th-century art is displayed throughout the house. Open Wednesday to Sunday, 10am to 6pm.
Via Mozart 14, T 02 7634 0121, www.casemuseomilano.it

12.00 Erastudio

This Brera-based gallery is spread across an early 20th-century building renovated under the direction of its owner, architect Patrizia Tenti. The exhibition spaces are divided into two areas: a former apartment on the third floor (above); and stables in the courtyard, which have been left untouched. Tenti's aim was to emphasise a number of the building's original features, in particular the window panes, shutters and door handles. The walls have been left bare to allow visitors to view the intriguing doodles of previous residents from the 1900s through to the 1950s. Exhibitions showcase international designers and architects; recent displays have included the work of Vincenzo De Cotiis, designer of Straf hotel (see p018). *Via Palermo 5, T 02 3919 8515, www.erastudio.it*

15.00 Fondazione Vico Magistretti

Milanese architect and designer Vico Magistretti was a major figure of 20th-century Italian design. In the 1940s and 1950s, he contributed to plans for the experimental neighbourhood QT8 on the edge of the city, as well an estate for Pirelli workers. In product design, he focused on functional furniture that could be mass produced, creating classics such as the 'Carimate' chair for Cassina. The studio where he worked for 60 years is now open to visitors, and offers two design excursions: one is a tour of 14 of his most important buildings in Milan; the other comprises visits to companies affiliated with the designer. Open Tuesdays (2pm-6pm), Thursdays (2pm-8pm), and Saturdays by appointment (2pm-6pm). *Via Conservatorio 20, T 02 7600 2964, www.vicomagistretti.it*

20.00 Il Salumaio di Montenapoleone
A renowned deli since 1957, Il Salumaio
opened this restaurant and a café in
the former stables of Palazzo Bagatti
Valsecchi in 2011. Expect simple, classic
food: a selection of cheeses, the finest
salami, fresh pasta, and veal cutlet in
breadcrumbs. In summer, reserve a table
in the courtyard under the lemon tree.
*Via Santo Spirito 10/Via Gesù 5. T 02 7600
1123, www.ilsalumaiodimontenapoleone.it*

URBAN LIFE
CAFÉS, RESTAURANTS, BARS AND NIGHTCLUBS

The city boasts many fine *pasticcerie* that double up as cafés, such as Pasticceria Cucchi (Corso Genova 1, T 02 8940 9793), in which you can enjoy Milan's favourite hot drink, *caffè*. Breakfast is usually a cappuccino and a brioche taken standing up at the bar. Avoid ordering a cappuccino after lunch, unless you want to be openly sneered at by the staff (it's strictly macchiato from midday on).

No time for a long lunch? Visit a bakery and fill up on focaccia or pizza by the slice. Pizzeria Spontini (Viale Papiniano 43, T 02 8366 0098) is a first-rate choice, as is a gelato from Shockolat (Via Giovanni Boccaccio 9, T 02 4810 0597) or Grom (Via Santa Margherita 16, T 02 8058 1041). Remember that many fashion stores have a café/restaurant; try Trussardi alla Scala (see p053) and Emporio Armani Caffè (Via Croce Rossa 2, T 02 7231 8680).

The Milanese are light drinkers who nurse their cocktails while snacking. Savour a classic *aperitivo* experience at Bar Basso (Via Plinio 29, T 02 2940 0580), ordering a *sbagliato* (Campari with sweet vermouth and prosecco), which was invented in the bar. For dinner, stalwarts include Bice (Via Borgospesso 12, T 02 7600 2572), Ristorante Da Giacomo (see p046) and Alla Cucina delle Langhe (Corso Como 6, T 02 655 4279). In many of the traditional restaurants, such as Alla Collina Pistoiese (see p049), the decor won't have changed much in years but the food will be top-notch. *For full addresses, see Resources.*

Erba Brusca

In an idyllic spot south of the city centre, this refreshingly modern restaurant was designed by Milan-based Rgastudio, who have channelled the spirit of its canalside location in a bright, airy interior. Erba Brusca's founder, Alice Delcourt, was born in France and raised in the US, but has long harboured a passion for Italy and its food. She honed her culinary skills working in several restaurants before striking out on her own in 2011. The venue has a charming rural dimension that includes a vegetable garden, but its overall ambience and food are wholly sophisticated. Local produce appears in dishes such as tarte tatin with aubergine, tomatoes and *stracciatella*. Diners can hire bicycles to ride along the Naviglio canal. Open Wednesday to Sunday. *Alzaia Naviglio Pavese 286, T 02 8738 0711, www.erbabrusca.it*

Ratanà

As a place to sample classic Italian fare in a contemporary setting, Ratanà is ideal. Beef carpaccio with balsamic vinegar sauce, Milanese risotto with saffron, and a luxurious panna cotta are some of the highlights of Cesare Battisti's concise menu, which is partnered by a well-planned wine list. Housed in an early 20th-century palazzina, which formed part of one of the first railway stations in Milan, the dining room offers an authentic but modern take on the trattoria experience. The pared-back interior, which features oak flooring and grey metal panels, is the work of Rgastudio, the designers of Erba Brusca (see p041). We'd recommend Ratanà as a destination for *aperitivo* too, when it serves plenty of tasty Milanese nibbles.
Via Gaetano De Castillia 28,
T 02 8712 8855, www.ratana.it

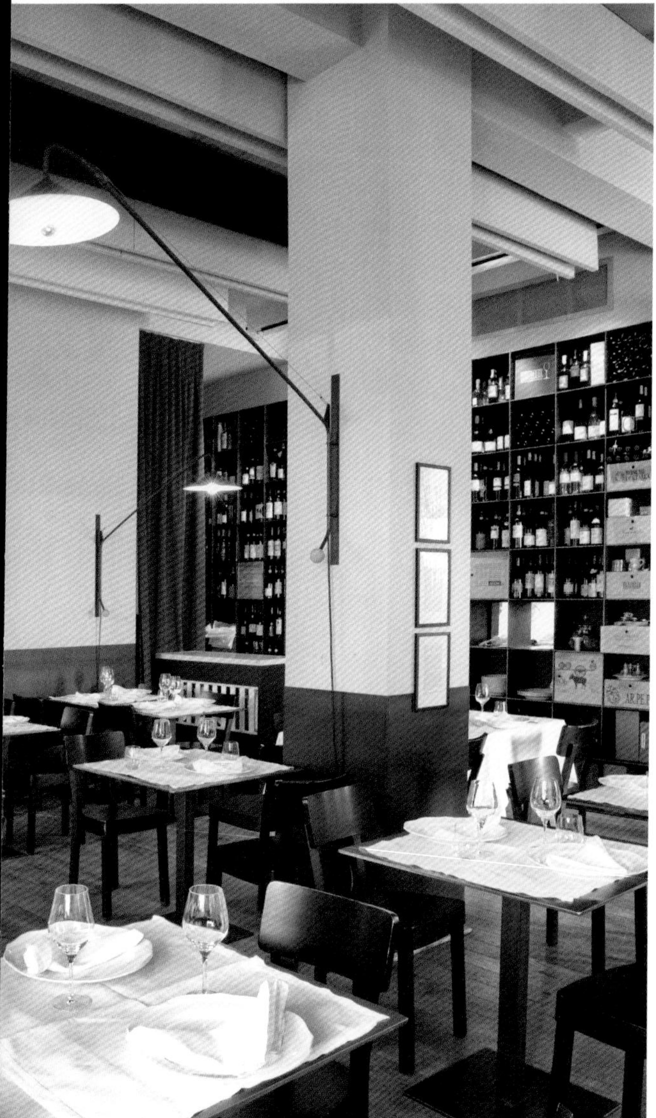

Pane e Acqua

This delightful venue on a residential street in Magenta is part of Spazio Rossana Orlandi (T 02 467 4471), one of Milan's best design galleries. Keen to provide a dining venue for her clients, Orlandi conjured up the idea for this restaurant, collaborating with architect Paola Navone on the interior – a blend of industrial elements (exposed cables, aluminium and raw brick), and salvaged and contemporary furniture, which is available to buy in the adjoining showroom. Mismatched chairs, quirky tableware and menus written inside well-thumbed novels make for a fun meeting place for coffee or lunch. The food, courtesy of chef Francesco Passalacqua, is equally delightful.
Via Matteo Bandello 14, T 02 4819 8622, www.paneacqua.com

Bistro Da Giacomo

Open from noon until midnight, this restaurant is a rarity in a city that likes to lunch precisely at 1pm and dines no earlier than 8pm. The menu also breaks the mould, presenting American fare like burgers and fries alongside Tuscan dishes, such as *pasta con funghi* and *costata alla fiorentina*. The venue is owned by the Bulleri family, who are behind well-known fish restaurant Da Giacomo (T 02 7602 3313), the Giacomo Arengario restaurant in Museo del Novecento (see p062), and Pasticceria Giacomo (T 02 7631 9147), which is situated just across the street and supplies Bistro Da Giacomo with its bread. In the evening, a mixture of politicians and fashion industry types bookend the bar, sipping on glasses of champagne.
Via Pasquale Sottocorno 6, T 02 7602 2653, www.giacomomilano.com

Il Baretto al Baglioni

Truthfully, we preferred Il Baretto's original location on Via Sant'Andrea, where it opened as an American bar in the early 1960s. However, now housed inside the Carlton Hotel Baglioni, the restaurant remains a favourite choice for lunch (when the clientele is made up of the CEOs of top design houses), dinner or an après-shopping *aperitivo*; those in the know use the door at Via della Spiga 6. The cheese and truffle toasts and crudités are delicious, and the ideal accompaniment to a glass of barolo or a flute of prosecco. Il Baretto is open every day, which can be handy when everything else in town is closed. For a gentle stroll before or after you arrive, the landscaped park, Giardini di Villa Comunale, is a stone's throw away. *Carlton Hotel Baglioni, Via Senato 5, T 02 781 255, www.baglionihotels.com*

Ristorante Alla Collina Pistoiese

This Tuscan restaurant is located in the densely packed, cobblestoned district between Via Torino and Corso Italia, which is a pleasant area to explore on foot. The venue dates back to 1938, when it was opened by Pietro Gori. Today, the restaurant is run by the third and fourth generations of the same family. The menu comprises classics from the Tuscany region – crostini, soups, pasta and plenty of meat. The Florentine steak is one of Alla Collina Pistoiese's most popular dishes, and the grilled fish is also excellent. In summer, order prosciutto with figs; in winter, try the *insalata di carciofi* (baby artichoke salad with parmesan and celery). The restaurant is closed on Fridays and Saturdays at lunchtime.
Via Amedei 1, T 02 8645 1085,
www.allacollinapistoiese.com

Dopolavoro Bicocca
Home of the Pirelli complex until the late
1980s, the Bicocca district has since been
transformed. Architect Vittorio Gregotti
was central to this, his projects including
HangarBicocca (T 02 6611 1573), an art
museum housed in a former factory. Its
industrial bistro Dopolavoro is a good
pitstop for lunch or a snack. It also serves
cocktails, Thursday to Sunday from 7pm.
Via Chiese 2, T 02 643 1111

Ama.mi

Located on one of Milan's major arteries, amid the *movida* of Sempione, this bar is a modish option for *aperitivo*. Donata Micetta's golden-hued interior combines custom-made wenge-wood furniture, marble and leather to great effect. Ama. mi (which means 'love me' or, in this case, 'love Milano') is subtly lit and snug without feeling claustrophobic. The clientele is a spirited but grown-up mix of thirty- and fortysomething locals; a younger crowd arrives on Friday and Saturday nights, when DJs enliven proceedings later in the evening. For a *passeggiata*, head south down Corso Sempione towards the park. You'll pass by the neoclassical Arco della Pace, Milan's triumphal arch, on the site of the old Roman walls of the city.
Corso Sempione 7, T 02 3453 0390, www.amamilano.com

Trussardi alla Scala

In the heart of Milan's theatre district, Café Trussardi is an insider's haunt, and perfect for drinks or dinner if you're planning to see a performance at La Scala (T 02 88 791), which is next door. A chic set arrives to sip prosecco beneath botanist Patrick Blanc's lush planting (above), or dine in the upstairs restaurant, helmed by Luigi Taglienti, who was sous chef here while Andrea Berton developed the unique style of contemporary Italian cuisine that earned Trussardi two Michelin stars. Taglienti has ensured that the menu still abounds with intricate combinations of flavour and texture, through dishes like lobster with purple potatoes, white peach and sangria sorbet, followed by liquid chocolate, cacao and mascarpone cheese. *Piazza della Scala 5, T 02 8068 8201, www.trussardiallascala.it*

INSIDER'S GUIDE

GUGLIELMO MIANI, CHIEF EXECUTIVE OFFICER

Head of luxury fashion brand Larusmiani and president of the Via Montenapoleone Association, Guglielmo Miani truly represents the spirit of Milan. The Larusmiani store has been in its present location (Via Montenapoleone 7, T 02 7600 6957) since 1954.

A good espresso at Conti Cafè (Via Montenapoleone 19, T 02 7639 4934) or Sant'Ambroeus (Corso Matteotti 7, T 02 7600 0540), is a typical start to Miani's day. Then his ideal tour would include the 18th-century Palazzo Morando (Via Sant'Andrea 6, T 02 8846 5933), Biblioteca Ambrosiana library (Piazza Pio XI 2, T 02 806 921) and, of course, Via Montenapoleone, for the chicest shopping in town. Here, he recommends renowned stores such as Vetrerie di Empoli (No 22, T 02 7600 8791), G Lorenzi (see p069), and Cusi (Corso Monforte 21-23, T 02 795 832) for its beautiful jewellery. His secret design addresses include L'Eclettico (Via San Gregorio 39, T 02 6707 9142) and Flaim di Riccardo (Via San Rocco 8).

For the ritualistic *aperitivo*, Miani prefers five-star hotels such as Armani (see p026), and suggests a stop at Camparino (Piazza Duomo 21, T 02 8646 4435), a historic bar managed by his own family for 50 years. Afterwards, Il Salumaio di Montenapoleone (see p038) is his first choice for dinner. Villa D'Este (Via Regina 40, Cernobbio, T 03 13 481), where he can unwind while admiring the landscape of Lake Como, is a perfect escape from the city. *For full addresses, see Resources.*

ARCHITOUR

A GUIDE TO MILAN'S ICONIC BUILDINGS

It should be said that Milan is not Italy's first port of call for the veteran architourist. Aside from the Duomo (see p014) – which took 400 years to complete and runs the gamut of styles, from Gothic to Renaissance – and its idiosyncratic neighbour, Torre Velasca (see p011), Milan's architectural pleasures are rather understated.

Plans are underway, however, for some ambitious regeneration schemes and Expo 2015. Architects who have contributed to the Expo's masterplan include Jacques Herzog, William McDonough and Stefano Boeri, whose Bosco Verticale dominates the newly created Porta Nuova district (see p009). CityLife is a residential and business development taking shape in the old trade-fair grounds in the north-west of Milan which, by 2014, will include skyscrapers by Arata Isozaki, Daniel Libeskind and Zaha Hadid. Just outside the city, in Rho-Pero, is the Fiera Milano complex (see p059), designed by Massimiliano and Doriana Fuksas.

Milan's architectural hero is Gio Ponti, whose Pirelli Tower (see p010) was a masterstroke of modern design. The former tenants, Lombardy's regional government, may have relocated to Palazzo Lombardia (see p058), but 'Il Pirellone' remains a potent symbol of the city. Next to the Duomo, Museo del Novecento (see p062) has proved to be one of Milan's most successful contemporary projects, along with Tadao Ando's Teatro Armani (Via Bergognone 59). *For full addresses, see Resources.*

Chiesa di San Francesco al Fopponino

The Pirelli Tower (see p010) is Gio Ponti's best-known building in Milan, where he worked all his life, but his contribution to the city includes other notable works: the twin office buildings (Via Moscova 3/Largo Donegani 2) built in 1936 and 1951 for the Montecatini company, and two striking churches. Chiesa di San Francesco, a collaboration with Antonio Fornaroli and Alberto Rosselli, was completed in 1964.

The facade is clad in diamond-shaped tiles and set back from the street, with the east and west wings recessed further, providing a screen to enclose the courtyards behind. The tiles and hexagonal windows are typical Ponti forms; those to the left and right of the nave are open, framing the sky. Ponti's Chiesa dell'Ospedale San Carlo, finished in 1967, is on Via Papa Pio. *Via Paolo Giovio 41, www.fopponino.it*

Palazzo Lombardia

Architects Pei Cobb Freed & Partners submitted the winning entry in a global competition to design Lombardy's new government headquarters. Completed in 2011, the curvilinear Palazzo Lombardia complex incorporates an array of open, interconnected spaces, the largest of which is protected from the elements by a transparent roof. The kingpin is a slender 160m high-rise, which was the tallest building in Milan before it was overtaken by Cesar Pelli's 230m Torre Garibaldi in Porta Nuova. Tradition dictates that a Madonnina (small gold-plated statue of the Madonna) be placed at the highest points in the city, to protect and oversee it. The original is on the top of the Duomo (see p014) and, in 2010, a copy was installed on Palazzo Lombardia.
Piazza Città di Lombardia 1

Fiera Milano

A 40-minute metro ride from the city centre, Massimiliano and Doriana Fuksas' 2005 trade-fair complex was part of a massive regeneration project. Built on the site of an old oil refinery, it covers a vast 570,000 sq m, and was constructed over a period of just 24 months at a cost of €715m. The structure's central element is a ribbon-like glass-and-steel canopy that stretches for 1.5km, enveloping the buildings along its path. It ends in a crater-like vortex at either side. A variety of innovative solutions were devised to help keep the site as green as possible. Most interesting is the photocatalytic paint used to treat the pavilions: the 100,000 sq m of painted surfaces neutralise the air pollution produced by 30,000 cars.
Strada Statale del Sempione 28,
www.nuovosistemafieramilano.it

Università Luigi Bocconi
Completed in 2008 and designed by
Dublin-based Grafton Architects, this
university faculty garnered the inaugural
World Architecture Festival's Building of
the Year award, and was described as a
'magical subterranean realm'. Its central
feature is a sunken 1,000-seat theatre,
topped with light-filled offices, around
which lie terraces and courtyards.
Via Roberto Sarfatti 25

Museo del Novecento

Constructed to display Milan's collection of modern and contemporary art, this highly anticipated museum, launched in 2010, adjoins the fascist-era Palazzo dell'Arengario lining Piazza del Duomo. Architects Italo Rota and Fabio Fornasari conceived a discreet, light-filled structure, incorporating a spiral ramp that connects the subterranean level to a panoramic terrace overlooking the piazza, a covered walkway and an external staircase. This links neighbouring Palazzo Reale to the rooftop bar/restaurant, Giacomo Arengario (T 02 7602 3313), which was designed by architects Laura Sartori Rimini and Roberto Peregalli. The art exhibits are excellent, with particularly strong sections dedicated to the futurists, spatialism and Arte Povera. *Via Marconi 1, T 02 8844 4061, www.museodelnovecento.org*

SHOPPING

THE BEST RETAIL THERAPY AND WHAT TO BUY

The major attraction in Milan is the shopping, in particular the 'Quadrilatero' of Via Alessandro Manzoni, Via Montenapoleone, Via della Spiga and Via Sant'Andrea. Luxury brands Prada (see p068), Giorgio Armani (Via Montenapoleone 2, T 02 7600 3234), Valentino (Via Montenapoleone 20, T 02 7600 6182) and Fendi (Via Sant'Andrea 16, T 02 7602 1617) are all here. Squeeze in a visit to Gallo (Via Alessandro Manzoni 16b, T 02 783 602) to stock up on socks; Corto Moltedo (Via Santo Spirito 14, T 02 3668 3713) for chic clutch bags; Tadao Ando's store for Duvetica (Via Santo Spirito 22, T 02 7602 2967); and the Herno flagship (Via della Spiga 1, T 02 9443 2789). On the edge of the Quadrilatero, Vionnet, currently under the direction of Italian Matteo Marzotto, has opened its first shop in Milan (Corso Monforte 16, T 02 4968 2563).

For bespoke suits, make an appointment at Brioni (Via Gesù 3, T 02 7639 0086). Valextra (Via Alessandro Manzoni 3, T 02 9978 6060) has superb leather goods and luggage. Via Durini specialises in furniture from the likes of B&B Italia (No 14, T 02 764 441), and Via Brera is the location of charming stores such as Anna Maria Consadori (see p077). Vintage hounds should trawl the antiques market held on the last Sunday of each month along the Naviglio Grande canal. It sells a variety of wares, from furniture and clothes to watches. Nearby bars and restaurants usually stay open all day. *For full addresses, see Resources.*

Ceccotti Collezioni

Founded by Aviero Ceccotti, this furniture company's origins date back to the 1950s. Ceccotti Collezioni was inaugurated much more recently, during the 2011 Salone del Mobile, in this 200 sq m showroom designed by Vincenzo de Cotiis. Spread across two floors of a former warehouse, the space is unashamedly minimal – stark white walls, concrete columns, aluminium fixtures. The contemporary furniture and lighting, curated by Franco Ceccotti and Massimo Castagna, places an emphasis on sustainable materials and exemplary craftsmanship. Yuni Ahn, Studio Drift, Noé Duchaufour-Lawrance, Jaime Hayon and Christophe Pillet are among the designers who have worked with Ceccotti, and some of the pieces are bespoke or handmade. *Via Gastone Pisoni 2, T 02 655 2750, www.ceccotticollezioni.it*

Dada Meeting Point
After opening shops in China and Salò on
Lake Garda, globetrotter, art collector
and interior designer Jamil Dada landed in
Milan. His store, an atmospheric boutique
carved out of a former convent, sells a
blend of new and vintage design, and less
obvious fashion labels. Look out for pieces
by Simone Rocha, Lucas Nascimento,
Corrado de Biase and ETS Callatay's shoes.
Via Gian Giacomo Mora 12, T 02 5810 5634

Prada

This is where it all began. The first Prada store, inside Galleria Vittorio Emanuele II (see p013), was opened in 1913 as a seller of leather goods by Mario Prada, Miuccia's grandfather. Although subtly enlarged over the past few years, the shop retains many original features, such as the Belgian marble floor, and mahogany and brass furniture. There are four other Prada stores in Milan. The Via Montenapoleone outlets sell menswear (No 6, T 02 7602 0273) and women's ready-to-wear (No 8, T 02 777 1771); the shop on Via della Spiga (No 18, T 02 780 465), designed by Roberto Baciocchi, focuses on women's accessories; and the branch on Corso Venezia (No 3, T 02 7600 1426) carries the sporty Linea Rossa collection and takes bespoke orders. *Galleria Vittorio Emanuele II 63-65, T 02 876 979, www.prada.com*

G Lorenzi

Long established as a master *coltellinaio* (cutler), G Lorenzi started trading in 1929. These days, its stock extends far beyond traditional knives, cutlery and scissors. This is where you will find the perfect tools to slice prosciutto, parmesan or truffles, or to achieve grooming perfection with the brand's comprehensive range of handmade Makassar ebony brushes, nail scissors, shoehorns, razors and mirrors. Ask to be shown one of the items on display and you'll soon find yourself confronted with hundreds more, which are locked away in drawers. Among the store's numerous treasures is this rather fabulous compact espresso-maker set (above), from €1,150, which plugs into the dashboard of your car for on-the-road use.
Via Montenapoleone 9, T 02 7602 2848, www.lorenzi.it

Villa Meissen

The 300-year-old Meissen porcelain company chose Milan as the location of its new European flagship, opening this showroom in one of the city's foremost villas. Painstakingly restored for the launch, the 16th-century Casa Carcassola-Grandi on Via Montenapoleone is replete with certain listed architectural features, including a neoclassical facade designed in the early 19th century by architect Nicola Dordoni, ceiling frescoes and a striking entrance portal by Gio Ponti. The company's historic porcelain, first created in the German region of Saxony in the early 1700s, is displayed alongside more contemporary product lines, such as fine jewellery and Meissen Home, a range of furnishings inspired by some of the designs held in the company's archives. The products are arranged across eight themed rooms, covering some 350 sq m.
Via Montenapoleone 3, www.meissen.com

Excelsior

This seven-floor department store, which opened in 2011, occupies a former cinema overlooking Galleria del Corso. The external architecture features a series of video displays and neon lighting, and is the work of Jean Nouvel and Italian architect Monica Armani; Vincenzo de Cotiis was responsible for the interiors. Although the facade may be off-puttingly brash, the interior is worth exploring for its democratic and extensive range of fashion, from Rag & Bone to Balmain, its accessories and homewares, and its impressive food and wine section, which is on the basement level. Excelsior is a very different environment from the venerable La Rinascente (opposite), which is nearby, but it certainly deserves a tour. *Galleria del Corso 4, T 02 7630 7301, www.excelsiormilano.com*

La Rinascente

In the mid-1800s, the Bocconi brothers started selling ready-to-wear clothes in Milan, a retail innovation for the time. La Rinascente grew out of this venture, and was established as a department store in its present location in 1917. The pioneering shop has collaborated with several design luminaries over the years, with the aim of promoting good, mass-produced Italian design. A 2012 refurbishment added some oomph to the third and fourth floors. The clothing and interiors departments retain an Italian focus, the basement is ideal for stationery, lighting and kitchenwares, and the food hall is not be missed. The restaurant (T 02 885 2471) is a highlight, with its sweeping outdoor terrace and unrivalled views of the Duomo (see p014). *Via Santa Radegonda 3, T 02 88 521, www.rinascente.it*

Wait and See
Uberta Zambeletti's boutique reflects her varied career as an interior designer, fashion stylist and art director. Tucked down a street lined with cafés and antiques shops, it sells women's apparel and vintage items, and a few accessories for men and children. Brands are rotated frequently, so regular shoppers should spy something interesting.
Via Santa Marta 14, T 02 7208 0195

Gianvito Rossi

This elegant shoe store is on the ground floor of Museo Bagatti Valsecchi (T 02 7600 6132), a 19th-century palazzo-turned-museum packed with art and decorative objects collected by its former owners, Fausto and Giuseppe Bagatti Valsecchi. The Rossi brand, launched in 2006, is produced exclusively in San Mauro Pascoli, an area of Emilia-Romagna renowned for its artisanal shoe and leather-making traditions. Designed by Patricia Urquiola, the chic boutique's interior is largely inspired by the architecture of its host; its four rooms are decorated in a palette of bronze, powder-pink and plum, with furnishings from Moroso and De Padova (see p078). Perch on a velvet divan while you ponder the perfect pair of heels.
Via Santo Spirito 7, T 02 7628 0988,
www.gianvitorossi.com

Anna Maria Consadori Gallery

Daughter of the Italian painter Silvio Consadori, Anna Maria trained as an architect before opening this showroom displaying Italian design from the 1930s onwards. Her taste is impeccable; pieces on sale have included sculptures by Gio Pomodoro and Mario Negri, expressionist ceramics by Lucio Fontana, paintings by Roberto Crippa and chairs by Giulio Minoletti. Consadori's father taught at the nearby Accademia di Bella Arti di Brera, housed in the 17th-century Palazzo Brera. Call in to visit one of the city's best museums, Pinacoteca di Brera (T 02 7226 3264), which exhibits an important collection of Italian paintings, covering the 13th to the 20th centuries and including works by Caravaggio and Tintoretto. *Via Brera 2, T 02 7202 1767, www.galleriaconsadori.com*

De Padova

This inspirational store produces and distributes furniture and products by Italian designers of the calibre of Achille Castiglioni, Vico Magistretti (see p036) and Pierluigi Cerri, as well as promoting emerging talent, such as Belgian Xavier Lust and Japanese firm Nendo. With her late husband Fernando, Maddalena De Padova began selling furniture in the 1950s on Via Montenapoleone, and has been introducing innovative ideas to the city ever since. The business relocated to the current shop on the corner of Corso Venezia and Via Senato in 1965. Making full use of the large windows, De Padova often asked Castiglioni to design the *allestimento* (display); he was also responsible for the store's makeover in 1986. It now has four floors, making the showroom one of the largest in Milan.
Corso Venezia 14, T 02 777 201, www.depadova.it

Azucena

Founded in 1947 by five architects, led by Luigi Caccia Dominioni, Azucena blazed a trail in interior design, utilising artisanal and new industrial production methods. Dominioni, Corrado Corradi Dell'Acqua, Ignazio Gardella, Maria Teresa and Franca Tosi had partly created the company to make furnishings for the houses they were designing and began producing a range of practical but beautiful products, such as Dominioni's 1954 'Cartuccia' wastepaper basket, €755, and umbrella stand, €945 (both above), made from black-iron sheet with polished brass and chrome-plated brass bands, respectively. In recent years, many original pieces have been enhanced with modern materials. The present shop may relocate; check the website for details. *Via della Passione 8, T 02 798 527, www.azucena.it*

Gay Odin

Among the antique jewellers that cluster around Corso Magenta is this artisanal chocolatier, whose original store opened in Naples in 1922. The Milan branch offers a taste of the Neopolitan delicacies, which are piled high in glass jars and displayed on wooden counters. Ignore the rather brusque service and take home some *peperoncino-cioccolato* (chilli chocolates) in one of the lovely boxes (above). If you have impending nuptials to attend, pick up a selection of traditional *cioccolatini confetti*, which come in a diverse variety of flavours – amaretto, limoncello, ricotta and pear, to name but a few. In spring or summer, try Gay Odin's unique *gelato foresta* – liquid chocolate served cold in a glass to be drunk at the counter.
Via San Giovanni sul Muro 19,
T 02 3966 3509, www.gay-odin.it

Le Stanze Di Dimore

Part gallery, part workshop, this former apartment on the second floor of an 18th-century palazzo near Brera is a distinctive backdrop for the creations of interior and product designers Emiliano Salci and Britt Moran. On display is a selection of their own furniture, as well as vintage artwork and objects gathered from around the globe.

Via Solferino 11, T 02 3653 7088,
www.dimorestudio.eu

Pirelli

This rubber-carpeted store is a fitting flagship for the groundbreaking Milanese brand, which was formed by engineer Giovanni Battista Pirelli in 1872. Designed by architect Renato Montagner, creative director of Pirelli's Pzero fashion range, the shop brings the company's products together under one roof for the first time, in an edgy 1,500 sq m space. Pzero clothing and footwear is displayed alongside cars and motorbikes sporting Pirelli tyres. As you might expect, innovations abound, from a soundproof wall to Robostock, the store's robotic stock keeper. One room displays items from the brand's archives, including advertising campaigns, photos and Bruno Munari's 'Meo Romeo' cat, designed by the artist for Pirelli in 1949. *Corso Venezia 1, T 02 6442 4242, www.pirellipzero.com*

Aspesi
Alberto Aspesi's womenswear has
become a Milan institution, cemented
by the opening of its first dedicated
store. Conceived by Antonio Citterio and
Partners in collaboration with London-
based art director Dirk Van Dooren of
creative agency Tomato, the 800 sq m
space is an attraction all of its own.
*Via Montenapoleone 13, T 02 7602 2478,
www.aspesi.com*

SPORTS AND SPAS

WORK OUT, CHILL OUT OR JUST WATCH

Milan's fitness culture has improved in recent years, although the city's gyms would struggle to compete with those in London, LA or New York; Downtown (Piazza Diaz 6, T 02 863 1181) is one of the best options. Yoga is starting to gain a following too, and a good studio is BeYoga (Via Carlo Botta 8, T 02 546 5590). Joggers should head to Parco Sempione, behind Castello Sforzesco (see p009), or Giardini Pubblici di Porta Venezia, although you might need to run around it several times to get a proper workout.

Not surprisingly, in a city obsessed with looks, there are plenty of options when it comes to pampering – Milan's fashion designers were early adopters of spa culture. Gianfranco Ferré has an ESPA (Via Sant'Andrea 15, T 02 7601 7526) next to his boutique, and the Bulgari Spa (Via Privata Fratelli Gabba 7b, T 02 805 805 200) offers treatments in glorious surroundings, as does Armani (see p092). Designer spas are not the only ones proliferating in the city. Culti Day Spa (Via Angelo Mauri 5, T 02 4851 7588) is a stylish sanctuary in Magenta, and Violette (Via Panfilo Castaldi 20, T 02 2951 9283) is one of Milan's few professional nail bars. For blow-dries or a trim, the fashion set head to salon Area 6 (Corso Concordia 6, T 02 3656 6257), run by the charismatic Alessandro Lisi. Italy's first medical spa, Istituto Image (Viale Bianca Maria 24, T 02 781 628), aims to boost both physical and mental wellbeing. *For full addresses, see Resources.*

Alfonso

Signor Franceschetti has been wielding a pair of scissors and a razor since he was 15 years old, and he opened this namesake barbershop some five decades ago, close to Milan's law courts. As a result, judges and barristers are frequent visitors to these chairs, as is any gentleman who desires a traditional cut or a perfectly executed close shave. Alfonso has many haircuts in his repertoire (he'd even do a mohawk on request, he tells us), but his favourite is 'the Italian', a style originating from the 1940s, in which the hair is closely trimmed at the back and sides but longer on top – think Marcello Mastroianni. When the grooming is complete, treat yourself at another Milan institution, nearby Taveggia (T 02 7628 0856), which has been making delectable *pasticcini* since 1909.
Via Cesare Battisti 8, T 02 551 2931

Piscina Cozzi
This 1934 Olympic-size pool in a fascist building received a facelift in 2008, and the addition of contemporary fixtures re-established it as a popular venue. In fact, it can get impossibly crowded, so we recommend visiting early in the morning, or at lunchtime at the weekends, although opening hours are extended during the summer.
Viale Tunisia 35, T 02 659 9703

Armani Spa

Set on the eighth floor of the Armani
Hotel (see p026), this sleek 1,200 sq m
spa comes with a knockout panorama.
The fully equipped gym, five single
treatment cabins, couples' room, pool
area and space dedicated exclusively
to hand and foot treatments all have
floor-to-ceiling louvred windows that
drink in Milan – this may be the only
location in the city where you can work
out while examining the architectural
intricacies of the Duomo (see p014), or
relax in an infinity pool while studying
the city skyline. Muted tones, green
river stone, understated tatami and
olive leather on the walls keep the
surroundings unmistakably 'Armani'.
Note that the spa is based on a particular
principle: you buy time, not a treatment.
It's open every day, from 9am to 9pm.
*Via Alessandro Manzoni 31, T 02 8883
8888, www.armanihotels.com*

Spa at Four Seasons

The exposed brickwork and vaulted ceilings of this 600-year-old nunnery make architect Patricia Urquiola's labyrinthine spa a deeply atmospheric proposal. The designer chose traditional Italian materials such as ceramic, durmast oak and travertine, then embellished them with lasers, carving or serigraphy to give the 800 sq m space a distinctive, contemporary feel. The serene retreat offers a range of massage, facial, body and nail treatments in seven rooms. Try the Caviar Body Treatment, which uses caviar pearls to nourish and firm the skin. There's a Turkish bath with a sauna and whirlpool, and a fitness centre and lap pool for the more energetic. The spa is open every day, 7am to 10pm.
Via Gesù 6-8, T 02 7708 1100,
www.fourseasons.com/milan/spa

ESCAPES

WHERE TO GO IF YOU WANT TO LEAVE TOWN

The Milanese take full advantage of the city's proximity to the Italian lakes, the Alps and the coast, and many of them spend practically every weekend out of town. The lakes offer the quickest escape. Como is a mere 40-minute journey; as is Lugano, located on the other side of the border with Switzerland; and it takes just over an hour to arrive at Desenzano on Lake Garda. All of these resorts can be reached quite easily from Milan's Stazione Centrale. To the north-east, Bergamo (see p098) is a truly wonderful city to explore. Further afield, journey times from Milan to Rome have been halved by the high-speed Frecciarossa train, which travels to the capital in three hours, or to Bologna in just one.

For a swim in the sea, make your way to Santa Margherita or Portofino in Liguria, about two hours away; Paraggi, a little bay near Portofino, is a prime spot. Most beaches around here are private, so try Bagni Fiore (Via Paraggi a Mare 1, Santa Margherita, T 01 8528 4831), which offers excellent facilities. Portofino itself is an upmarket fishing village that boasts impressive shopping and fine restaurants. If you have a few days to spare, check into a mountain spa. Therme Vals (see p102) can be reached by car in three-and-a-half hours, or try the South Tyrol region for the Vigilius Resort (see p100) and Terme Merano (opposite). To visit either, take a train to Bolzano and then it's a 30km taxi ride.
For full addresses, see Resources.

Terme Merano, South Tyrol

Merano, in the Texal mountain basin, has a unique microclimate – enjoying 300 days of sunshine per year – and thermal baths designed by local architect Matteo Thun, something of a one-man wellbeing industry in the region (see p100). Spread over 7,500 sq m, Terme Merano's facilities include a total of 25 pools, which can be found both indoors, under a giant glass cube, and outside, in lush parklands. The vast complex includes various saunas (mixed and swimwear-free), three steam baths, a caldarium, a gym and a vitality centre with 26 stylish rooms offering treatments using natural local ingredients. Thun also designed the 139-room Hotel Terme Merano (T 04 7325 9259), which has subterranean access to the baths. *Piazza Terme 9, Merano, T 04 7325 2000, www.termemerano.it*

GombitHotel, Bergamo

Clasped within defensive walls, Bergamo's old town has retained its medieval and 16th-century outline, nestled beneath the foothills of the Alps. Ancient buildings and a backdrop of mountains, valleys and plains make it easy to forget you're only 50 minutes from central Milan. Built flush against the 13th-century stone Torre del Gombito, the GombitHotel is the first design hotel within the walls of the *città alta* (upper city). The 13 rooms, whose interiors were designed by Gio Pozzi, are all unique but share a minimal aesthetic (Suite 14, above). Not only a place to sleep, Gombit aims to be an experimental gallery, where young artists create work for display, adding an artistic feel to public spaces such as the study area (opposite). *Via Mario Lupo 6, T 03 524 7009, www.gombithotel.it*

Vigilius Mountain Resort, Lana
Take a cable car to reach Matteo
Thun's 1,500m-high Vigilius Mountain
Resort, which sits in sublime isolation.
The service doesn't always match the
surroundings, but the hay-bath cure,
a therapy practised in the Dolomites
for centuries, really does work wonders
on circulation complaints and cellulite.
Vigiljoch, South Tyrol, T 04 7355 6600,
www.vigilius.it

Therme Vals, Vals, Switzerland

Milan's proximity to the Swiss border means that Therme Vals makes for a very pleasant car journey. Here, Peter Zumthor has used 60,000 slabs of Valser quartzite to create a cathedral to bathing, with indoor and outdoor thermal pools. The use of light and shade, and open and enclosed spaces, enhances the feeling of wellbeing as guests take in the health benefits of the spring. Book in advance for the wellness centre, which offers a varied range of treatments, from masks and exfoliation to wraps and massage. Stay at the interconnected Hotel Therme Vals (T +41 819 268 080), in one of the Zumthor-designed rooms, or at the excellent family guesthouse Hotel Alpina (T +41 819 207 040), where you should reserve a modernised room.
T +41 819 268 080, www.therme-vals.ch

NOTES
SKETCHES AND MEMOS

RESOURCES
CITY GUIDE DIRECTORY

A

Alfonso 089
Via Cesare Battisti 8
T 02 551 2931

Alla Cucina delle Langhe 040
Corso Como 6
T 02 655 4279
www.trattoriaallelanghe.com

Ama.mi 052
Corso Sempione 7
T 02 3453 0390
www.amamilano.com

Anna Maria Consadori Gallery 077
Via Brera 2
T 02 7202 1767
www.galleriaconsadori.com

Area 6 088
Corso Concordia 6
T 02 3656 6257

Armani Spa 092
Armani Hotel
Via Alessandro Manzoni 31
T 02 8883 8888
www.armanihotels.com

Aspesi 086
Via Montenapoleone 13
T 02 7602 2478
www.aspesi.com

Azucena 080
Via della Passione 8
T 02 798 527
www.azucena.it

B

B&B Italia 064
Via Durini 14
T 02 764 441
www.bebitalia.it

Bagni Fiore 096
Via Paraggi a Mare 1
Santa Margherita Ligure
Paraggi
T 01 8528 4831
www.bagnifiore.it

Bar Basso 040
Via Plinio 29
T 02 2940 0580
www.barbasso.com

Il Baretto al Baglioni 048
Carlton Hotel Baglioni
Via Senato 5
T 02 781 255
www.baglionihotels.com

BeYoga 088
Via Carlo Botta 8
T 02 546 5590
www.beyogacenter.it

Biblioteca Ambrosiana 054
Piazza Pio XI 2
T 02 806 921
www.ambrosiana.eu

Bice 040
Via Borgospesso 12
T 02 7600 2572
www.bicemilano.it

Bistro Da Giacomo 046
Via Pasquale Sottocorno 6
T 02 7602 2653
www.giacomomilano.com

Brioni 064
Via Gesù 3
T 02 7639 0086
www.brioni.it

HOTELS

ADDRESSES AND ROOM RATES

Hotel Alpina 103
Room rates:
double, from €180
Vals
Switzerland
T +41 819 207 040
www.hotel-alpina-vals.ch

Armani Hotel 026
Room rates:
double, from €605
Via Alessandro Manzoni 31
T 02 8883 8381
www.armanihotels.com

Bulgari Hotel 028
Room rates:
double, from €530;
Deluxe Suite, €650
Via Privata Fratelli Gabba 7b
T 02 805 8051
www.bulgarihotels.com

Foresteria Monforte 031
Room rates:
double, from €150;
Suite, from €180
Piazza del Tricolore 2
T 02 370 272
www.foresteriamonforte.it

Four Seasons 017
Room rates:
double, €600;
Suites 14, 16, 18 and 19, €2,530;
Renaissance Suite 115, €4,950
Via Gesù 6-8
T 02 77 088
www.fourseasons.com/milan

GombitHotel 098
Room rates:
double, from €200;
Suite 14, €450
Via Mario Lupo 6
Bergamo
T 03 524 7009
www.gombithotel.it

Grand Hotel et de Milan 024
Room rates:
double, from €680;
Suite Superior, €1,200
Via Alessandro Manzoni 29
T 02 723 141
www.grandhoteletdemilan.it

Mandarin Oriental 016
Room rates:
prices on request
Via Monte di Pietà
www.mandarinoriental.com

Palazzo Segreti 022
Room rates:
double, from €250;
Room 8, from €700
Via San Tomaso 8
T 02 4952 9250
www.palazzosegreti.com

Park Hyatt 025
Room rates:
double, from €570;
Room 205, €625;
Room 105, €815;
Diplomatic Suite, €3,930
Via Tommaso Grossi 1
T 02 8821 1234
www.milan.park.hyatt.com

Straf 018
Room rates:
double, from €230;
Standard Room, €350
Via San Raffaele 3
T 02 805 081
www.straf.it

3Rooms 019
Room rates:
double, €340;
Room 3, €340
Corso Como 10
T 02 626 163
www.3rooms-10corsocomo.com

Hotel Terme Merano 097
Room rates:
double, from €250
Piazza Terme 1
Merano
South Tyrol
T 04 7325 9259
www.hoteltermemerano.com

Hotel Therme Vals 103
Room rates:
double, from €260
Vals
Switzerland
T +41 819 268 080
www.therme-vals.ch

TownHouse Street Duomo 020
Room rates:
double, from €200;
Studio, from €200;
Two-bedroom Suite, €250
Via Santa Radegonda 14
T 02 8905 8297
www.townhouse.it

Vigilius Mountain Resort 100
Room rates:
double, from €315
Vigiljoch
Lana
South Tyrol
T 04 7355 6600
www.vigilius.it

Villa D'Este 054
Room rates:
double, from €505
Via Regina 40
Cernobbio
T 03 13 481
www.villadeste.com

Hotel Villa San Carlo Borromeo 030
Room rates:
double, from €150;
Suite, from €350
Piazza Borromeo 20
Senago
T 02 994 741
www.hotelvillasancarloborromeo.com

W 016
Room rates:
prices on request
Via Brera 19
T 02 63 361
www.starwoodhotels.com

WALLPAPER* CITY GUIDES

Executive Editor
Rachael Moloney

Author
Silvia Brambilla

Art Director
Loran Stosskopf
Art Editor
Eriko Shimazaki
Designer
Mayumi Hashimoto
Map Illustrator
Russell Bell

Photography Editor
Elisa Merlo
Assistant Photography Editor
Nabil Butt

Chief Sub-Editor
Nick Mee
Sub-Editors
Julia Chadwick
Greg Hughes

Editorial Assistant
Emma Harrison

Intern
Jessica Rusby

Wallpaper* Group Editor-in-Chief
Tony Chambers
Publishing Director
Gord Ray
Managing Editor
Jessica Diamond
Acting Managing Editor
Oliver Adamson

Contributors
Stephanie Epiro
Kerry Olsen

Wallpaper* ® is a registered trademark of IPC Media Limited

First published 2006
Revised and updated 2008, 2011 and 2013

© 2006, 2008, 2011 and 2013
IPC Media Limited

ISBN 978 0 7148 6461 7

All prices are correct at time of going to press, but are subject to change.

Printed in China

PHAIDON

Phaidon Press Limited
Regent's Wharf
All Saints Street
London N1 9PA

Phaidon Press Inc
180 Varick Street
New York, NY 10014

Phaidon® is a registered trademark of Phaidon Press Limited

www.phaidon.com

A CIP Catalogue record for this book is available from the British Library.

PHOTOGRAPHERS

Gabriele Basilico
Milan city view,
inside front cover

Beppe Brancato
Erastudio, p035

Vanni Burkhart
3Rooms, p019

**Gianluca Albertari/
Fotogramma**
Piscina Cozzi, pp090-091

Patrice Hanicotte
Pirelli Tower, p010
Torre Velasca, p011
Torre Branca, p012

Andrea Martiradonna
GombitHotel, p098, p099

Alberto Narduzzi
Galleria Vittorio
Emanuele II, p013
Foresteria Monforte, p031

Peartree Digital
G Lorenzi espresso-
maker set, p069
Gay Odin
chocolates, p081

Philippe Ruault
Fiera Milano, p059

Claudio Sabatino
Duomo, pp014-015
Four Seasons, p017
TownHouse Street
Duomo, pp020-021
Palazzo Segreti,
p022, p023
Bulgari Hotel, p028, p029
Pavè, p033
Villa Necchi
Campiglio, p034
Fondazione Vico
Magistretti, pp036-037
Il Salumaio di
Montenapoleone,
pp038-039
Erba Brusca, p041
Ratanà, pp042-043
Pane e Acqua, p044, p045
Bistro Da Giacomo,
pp046-047
Il Baretto
al Baglioni, p048
Dopolavoro Bicocca,
pp050-051
Ama.mi, p052
Guglielmo Miani, p055
Chiesa di San Francesco
al Fopponino, p057
Palazzo Lombardia, p058
Università Luigi
Bocconi, pp060-061
Museo del
Novecento, p062, p063
Dada Meeting
Point, pp066-067

Villa Meissen, pp070-071
Excelsior, p072
Wait and See, pp074-075
Anna Maria Consadori
Gallery, p077
Pirelli, p084, p085
Aspesi, pp086-087
Alfonso, p089

Filippo Thiella
Ceccotti Collezioni, p065

Gionata Xerra
Armani Spa, pp092-093

MILAN
A COLOUR-CODED GUIDE TO THE CITY'S HOT 'HOODS

MAGENTA
Leonardo da Vinci's *The Last Supper* finds itself in the most chichi part of town

SEMPIONE
This historic district of Milan, which includes a large park, is peppered with landmarks

ZONA DUOMO/GALLERIA
The city's most recognisable buildings have been joined by a bold new art museum

QUADRILATERO DELLA MODA
Shopping nirvana – if you can't buy it here, you probably can't buy it anywhere

BRERA
An interesting art and foodie scene is centred on the streets behind La Scala opera house

ZONA TORTONA
Always a focal point during the annual Salone del Mobile, this area is steadily on the rise

For a full description of each neighbourhood, see the Introduction.
Featured venues are colour-coded, according to the district in which they are located.